FABIAN GEYRHALTER

I0135196

THE BRAND THERAPY BOOK 2

By Fabian Geyrhalter

THE BRAND THERAPY BOOK 2

BRANDTRO PUBLISHING

5318 E 2nd St #888
Long Beach, CA 90803

ORDERING INFORMATION:

For details, contact the publisher at the address above or send an email to *orders@brandtro.com*

ISBN 978-1-7349397-1-2

Every possible effort has been made to ensure that the information in this book is accurate at the time of first publishing. The editor, publisher, or author cannot accept responsibility for damage or loss occasioned to any person acting or refraining from action as a result of the content of this publication.

This book, just like the first in the series, is dedicated to the brand builders around the world who understand that a brand is a living thing that requires daily attention and nurturing. And sometimes a kick in the butt.

TABLE OF CONTENTS

ABOUT THIS BOOK

Back in 2017, I composed an Instagram post in which I gave brand advice to my followers. Because it was a Thursday, I intuitively added the hashtag "#BrandTherapyThursday." And because I am a creature of habit, 113 Brand Therapy Thursday posts later, it turned into the first Brand Therapy book in 2020, a small but mighty physical book (which is not for anyone who does not like small books or large type) whose sole purpose is to inspire you, the reader, to keep pushing your or your clients' brand forward from a strategic, visual, or verbal point of view.

I haven't stopped writing these weekly thoughts, and at the very beginning of 2023 I realized I had generated enough therapeutic ideas on creating, activating, or transforming a brand that it was time to introduce the second chapter of this series.

Enjoy these prompts all in one go or one at a time, randomly or daily, as you work on your own brand or assist others in creating brands that strive to be the best they can be.

What is brand strategy? In its essence, it is not a business strategy; it is a strategy that relates to your brand, one step removed from business, one step closer to an authentic relationship with your specific audience or tribe, if I may use brand lingo. Brand strategy is crucial for any business, and the pointers on the following pages should empower you to align your venture or your clients' projects with your audience's needs and expectations.

FABIAN GEYRHALTER

BRAND STRATEGY

Branding makes you notice. Marketing provides you with value and proof points. And then branding hits in again to keep you engaged and delighted. And so the wondrous virtuous cycle of a brand begins.

Any company is purpose-driven by nature; otherwise, it would have no reason to exist. Let's ensure we dive deep to find a bigger emotional purpose that goes beyond the tactical problem a company helps solve through the ways in which it promotes, enables, or helps bridge a specific positive change for individuals, communities, or the planet.

The more global your consumer brand becomes, the more regional it needs to think and act.

Social media is not a thing your brand does. It is the most current version of your brand. It must be reviewed and assessed weekly and handled more carefully than your biggest marketing initiative.

So much can go wrong when you launch a new offering into the world: Your product may have flaws, your pricing strategy may backfire, or a pivot may be necessary. But if you create a brand people want to be a part of, if you stand for something your audience aligns with, perhaps even aches for, you are bigger than your offering. That is the incredible—and incredibly overlooked—power of branding for startups.

Never play it safe with your startup brand. Attract haters so lovers will follow multifold.

Predictability creates brands. Even innovation or transformation has to fall into a brand's predictability. An audience relies on the consistency of a brand, so clearly understanding your brand's DNA is crucial for any company to function on a true brand level.

As an author, once I have a book's outline down on a single page, the rest seems to come easily. The same is true for your brand: Once you have the core brand philosophy defined, then branding, culture, and sales will come easily thereafter.

If your brand takes a stance on a social movement, partake with heart and soul. Dedicate dollars and manpower to it. Treat it like a campaign without an end date. Only then will you create true change and gain your customers' trust and support in return.

If you study your competitors in order to reshape your brand, you will remain undifferentiated.

BRAND STRATEGY

The key ingredient to a lasting brand name and logo is foresight.

Let's not forget that every brand comprises a bunch of humans striving to create value for other humans. Is your brand continuously reflecting that fundamental idea, or is it trying so hard to be a brand that it leaves the human aspect behind?

The easier it is for others to copy your idea, the more significant branding becomes to the success and longevity of your venture.

No brand is perfect when it comes to sustainability, but if you show your audience how you are striving to be, you will gain trust and respect. This can be as simple as stating you are aware that your packaging is not recyclable and that you are actively working on changing that.

Pushing out marketing without a brand strategy in place is the tail wagging the dog.

The past decade was about doing good as a brand. And doing good was good enough. Today, brands need to activate their mission in ways that engage their audiences on a participatory level. How much have you supported a shared cause on behalf of my very own purchasing footprint with your brand? What part do I play in it?

Brand is the heart and soul of a company which is demonstrated through its visual and verbal atmosphere.

Imagine today's kids starting to use the word brand with admiration and a sparkle in their eyes as they grow up based on the companies we now passionately build and surround them with. Brands should be delightful experiences. They should be admired for innovation and the founders' grit. Changing the perception of this word should be our common goal as entrepreneurs and branding professionals.

That moment when fear turns into excitement:

Before a big presentation. Before a bungee jump. Before the release of your bold and honest campaign.

Make sure your brand is taking brave enough steps that scare the heck out of you until the moment of release when your tribe can feel that excitement.

If your brand's website has no "About Us" section, don't bother launching.

Social media displays your brand's often-forgotten yet most accessible focus group. All the insights about your audience, or the audience you aim to attract, are right in front of you, waiting to be tapped into.

If you are in a legacy B2B business with no real differentiators and have been competing on price alone for years, start looking within. Your company culture and employee retention may speak volumes about why to pick your firm over others. Good folks like working with other good folks. It may turn out to be your competitive advantage begging to be showcased.

Seamless UX

+

CX

=

Brand x^2

If the brand DNA of empowerment is at the heart of most brands today, why are shared revenue models and employee-owned business structures not a parallel trend?

Most commodity and legacy companies don't lack the budget, manpower, or marketing skills but simply the courage to go against the standards set by their own industry to truly stand out in the market space and capture the expectations, hearts, and minds of today's consumer.

How to fast-track your first product launch:

1. As a team, create clarity and focus on what your brand is and is not.

2. Establish an authentic brand voice, which comes easily after step 1.

3. Set up a simple yet distinct design language without overthinking it.

4. Do all the other things you would have done before reading this. A few more steps than you planned for, but they will create fans instantly while saving you time in the long term.

Do you know who is crucial for brand success? Human resources. If you have a high employee turnover rate, your customers will sense it. The same will happen if newly hired team members do not align with the brand's long-term vision. So make sure HR fully understands your branding and is involved as it periodically evolves.

Never trust a creative agency with more answers than questions on the initial call. Informed answers can only emerge after informed beginnings.

Cherished brands are not in the business of selling. They are in the business of sharing empathetic solutions their audiences ache for. Selling is the desired side effect of their relentless focus on the people they serve.

B2B, just like B2C, is People to People (P2P).

You can derive one thing from your brand early on that will not change regardless of the transformations you will face as a company: your brand's soul.

Uncover it. Own it. Live it. Share it.

Conducting brand research? Join Facebook Groups in your targeted niche (From accountants to zero -emissions vehicles) and ask questions. You will get unfiltered opinions of true fanatics at instant speeds and zero cost.

Allow curiosity to be the driver behind your brand: the curiosity of the founder to innovate, the curiosity of the brand-building team to go against the grain, and the curiosity of the intrigued audience to learn more.

Reduce your brand to the max. The more focused the positioning, the brand identity, and the messaging, the bigger the impact.

Brands rightfully spend a lot of time deriving who they are, but it's equally important for them to understand who they are not.

Would you rather dine at a restaurant with a huge menu that has something for everyone or go to the place that has the best X, where people line up and once they are sold out they close for the day? Yep, most of us get more excited about the second option. So what is the X that your brand offers? Is it time to focus in and double down?

Once you truly understand who you are as a brand—your brand DNA or essence—something magical happens: branding, marketing, and company culture all fall into place almost effortlessly, defined by a common ideology that is bigger than the company's commercial offering.

You can and should file trademarks and patents, but it will be hard to keep defending them when copycats start showing up. On the flip side, you can deliberately craft a brand with a unique vibe that people love, one you can safeguard and no one can copy. That is the sheer power of branding.

Brand differentiation can sometimes be as easy as shining a light on an important common truth your competitors have simply neglected in their brand narrative.

Why brand strategy must precede marketing efforts:

Think first, then act.

Even though we love to overthink it, branding is a lot like other complex creative endeavors. Just think of a great TV series: a story that is well thought out and engaging that feels new yet relatable. There is no scripted ending, so it can adjust over time. It is crafted for a specific audience and delivered through distinct, creative, and consistent execution.

The only risk of niching down is not committing 100% and going all the way.

Now that almost every company is wearing sustainability and purpose on their sleeves regardless of proof points, this is the time to focus on fostering a joyful and giving company culture. It can't be faked; your company will benefit, and your customers will feel and cherish it.

Every brand is created from the inside out and fueled from the outside in—a spark that ignites the fire that the audience keeps on fueling. Brand strategy helps some find that spark and helps others reignite it.

The power of high-end niche positioning? A $14,000 Specialized S-Works mountain bike comes without pedals. A $10,000 Mark Levinson VPI turntable comes without a cartridge (needle). It basically renders the products useless. It sounds absurd unless you are their audience, in which case it makes perfect sense because you want a choice in components. That is the power of connoisseur brands.

Advisory boards are essential for brands seeking diverse insights and perspectives that enable business growth. Adding a brand strategist to your board will ensure product development and marketing will always be in sync with the soul of your brand, which serves as the emotional connection to your audience.

B2B companies require B2C brand thinking to remain competitive in the long run.

If authenticity is what consumers seek in brands and your people are what fuels it, isn't it time to double down on company culture to make your brand come to life?

Fortune 500 companies can do many things; creating cult brands is not one of them. That is why deriving an authentic brand strategy is so important for startups. It can be their biggest competitive advantage from the get-go.

Why is brand experience so important for brand growth? Because most advertising is fake, as are influencers' paid opinions. What is left is people sharing brands because knowing about them enhances their own brand, especially in front of others. It is still the most honest way for brands to experience growth, and it is rooted in putting brand experience front and center.

Your consumer brand has direct and indirect competition. Now add beloved brands like Red Bull, Nike, and Patagonia to the list because today you are competing for attention with all other brands in your audience's social feeds. Brand, design, write, and act accordingly.

AI, with some human creative direction, will be able to replace almost all of the labor involved in the branding of your company, from naming to the creation of logos and beyond, within this decade. But it won't be capable of successfully uncovering and defining the positioning and DNA of your brand.

My most crucial and actionable brand tip for SAAS companies is this: you likely exist to make the complex simple and approachable, yet your site is a complex labyrinth of icons and industry jargon. Do your brand and your potential customers a favor and walk your talk by having your copy and design language showcase that brand promise of simplicity.

At first, your brand has its fist high up in the air with a big mission and lots of attitude. Then it slowly gets watered down one digital ad campaign and e-commerce site analysis at a time. Suddenly you find yourself middle of the road, catering to everyone and no one at all. Don't let data kill the soul of your brand.

Some will like and some will dislike your brand, but when you witness someone defending your brand, you'll know you have created a deep and lasting bond with your audience.

The letters ART are centered within STRATEGY. Coincidence? I doubt it. If you derive art out of strategy it turns into powerful communication design. A synergistic combination that is at minimum half as impactful if not explored together.

If you as a founder or CEO enjoy a sport and sponsor a leading athlete, remember that any brand partnership demands harmony with your brand's values and DNA. If the two don't sync naturally, it will not only cease to yield results but may also hurt your brand image.

Don't underestimate the importance of romance in branding. Associating small batch production, idyllic locations, or moving stories with your brand image will sway not only the dreamers.

Why is now the time for brands to lead with a bigger purpose? The next generation of employees aches to create a measurable impact that is bigger than their paychecks while the outgoing leadership desires to leave a lasting legacy that is bigger than their corporate history.

Brand strategy, in essence, is like using the magic of Jazz to eventually turn a cacophony into a symphony.

The Brand Cocktail Recipe:

1. 2 parts product/service
2. 2 parts brand story and soul
3. *Shake*
4. Share
5. Receive glowing feedback
6. Make new friends

Authenticity is without a doubt one of the most important brand traits desired today. As a large organization not used to showcasing your true selves, have Marketing collaborate with HR to derive and subsequently help showcase the true soul of your brand. Not a common yet very powerful collaboration.

BRAND STRATEGY

The word "corporate" has no more use in 2023 and beyond.

Let's act accordingly as brands and as brand builders.

Let's catapult it out of our mindsets and vocabulary once and for all.

How branding helps startups:

Idea stage
→ **Sets the strategic direction**

Launch stage
→ **Attracts the right tribe**

Growth stage
→ **Makes them fall in love**

Maturity stage
→ **Surprises and delights them**

Once a year, get your team together and envision what you would do differently if you were a well-funded but not yet known prelaunch startup in your space: you have the freedom to start over, innovate, brand, and market in any which way you deem appropriate. Collect the ideas and use the learnings to push your brand forward over the next 12 months.

Would your brand's humor resonate in a different country or culture? Forget focus groups. Instead, see what movies are trending there on Netflix. This will give you key insights into the tastes and mindsets of your new audience.

The journey from bland to brand takes one important first step: Uncovering what makes your company unique on a non-functional, but emotional level—and subsequently weaving that into everything you say and everything you do.

Uncertain times are certainly great for new brand launches. Seems illogical, but as most others will put their brand introductions on hold while waiting for things to get better, you will face less competition and noise in the marketplace. That, in turn, creates more thirst in consumers to engage with new brands and products like yours.

Branding a two-sided marketplace where both audiences are equally as important to your success yet they receive different functional benefits? Uncover the most important joined emotional benefit and have that be the focal point of your branding.

Which is easier: conveying ongoing trust as a business-to-business (B2B) brand or sharing occasional delight as a consumer brand? Yeah, my point exactly. It is time to acknowledge how crucial a role branding plays in B2B environments.

The brand bible is dead and it's not blasphemy. Today's brands should have strategic, visual, and verbal guiding principles that function as the brand's throughline which must continuously evolve with the brand, its audience, and market space.

Make your brand guide your frenemy. Follow along religiously for brand consistency but break out rebelliously at times to innovate and push the brand forwards.

Many startup founders don't believe they need to invest in branding early on, yet all they ache for is to have super fans. Well, crap brand, no super fans, it's as simple as that.

Branding for startups is a lot like the coming of age for teenagers. Lots of distractions during the pre-launch and launch phases (puberty) make for hasty on-the-fly decisions, but once the growth stage is entered suddenly the desire for an unmistakable personality, a refined image, a deeper purpose, a close-knit community, and empathy start to emerge.

BRAND STRATEGY

Send out the right vibe
to attract the right tribe.

As a legacy company with a far from sexy or tech-forward offering, don't try to pretend you are competing on innovation with the new players in your category. Instead, double down on being the old school brand one came to rely on for when it matters.

A company's look and feel are so much more than meets the eye. They encompass a strategic move that is consistently applied across all touchpoints to draw you into a brand. They are the first features anyone sees. The pointers on the following pages will assist you in treating your company's visual strategy with the respect it deserves.

VISUAL CLARITY

Your brand's name and logo are like the hook of a chart-topping pop song. Your brand goes deep, but the verbal and visual hook must be instantaneous and memorable so even a young child can easily recall it. It's what makes a hit a hit in music, just like in branding.

You cannot create an iconic logo, but you can build an iconic brand. If that brand has been equipped with a unique, simple, and memorable logo, it too can turn iconic, but it lives in a symbiotic relationship the brand needs to lead.

VISUAL CLARITY

Stock photography has incredible powers: It can almost instantaneously create bland brands. Carefully adjust it to your brand design language and only use it in emergencies, such as budget or time crunches.

Most brand guides are useless because they overwhelm clients and aren't actionable. On top of that, many interdepartmental company communications are broken; hence the guides—and subsequently the brands—are never successfully and succinctly activated, which is the sole goal of any (re)branding effort. Instead, short, simple, organic, and collaborative brand overview documents are destined to craft better brands from the start and over time.

VISUAL CLARITY

If you are testing out your startup idea by creating an MVP, you may want to settle for an MVB to go along with it: a minimal viable branding. Something that is not bold in colors and design. Enough to support you without sticking in people's heads. Just a name and identity that gets you to the place of full commitment, at which point you should invest in getting it perfectly right, both the product and the brand.

Your company's logo is the purest expression of your brand's soul.

VISUAL CLARITY

Logos are not art. On the contrary, they are visual identifiers that communicate through their striking simplicity. The fewer elements they use to convey a concept, the better they will work. Great logos are so memorable anyone should be able to replicate their essence with a pen and paper and 30 seconds of spare time.

Great B2B logo designs handle two very opposing jobs flawlessly: they blend in with the rest of the industry yet boldly stand out from the competition.

VISUAL CLARITY

Timeless is the ultimate cool—in branding and in life.

In times where we thankfully squash stereotypes across the board, let's squash the "B2B brands are not sexy" stereotype once and for all.

VISUAL CLARITY

A rebrand offers a unique chance for a company's branding to become more aspirational than the actual product or service. Not being bold enough or not thinking big enough to visually and verbally capture that chance is a huge missed opportunity.

Logo-wear renaissance! Instead of giving your cheap logo shirts to employees who cringe wearing them while gardening, outfit loyal fans with high-quality and fashionable branded clothes instead. They will embody them, and you will actually see a return on your inexpensive brand investment. Call it influencer marketing, if you must.

VISUAL CLARITY

Creating a brand name and logo are linear processes. However, unlike developing your brand, which takes years and is organic and intrinsic to an extent, when it comes to these crucial foundational brand elements, it is all about trusting the methods of professionals.

White space in design is like pauses in a speech: it allows the content to sink in and make the impact more effective.

VISUAL CLARITY

With a logo redesign, you must learn not to focus on the opinions and chatter immediately after launch and instead have a strong vision and foresight for implementation and strategic rollout where the brand truly comes to life. It takes discipline, but the time after the immediate launch is usually the time that matters the least for the brand long term.

Branding for your early-stage startup is like investing in a captivating trailer for the movie you envision sharing with your audience down the road.

VISUAL CLARITY

What is the power of great visual identity design driven by a differentiated brand strategy? Most of today's new companies have their core purpose centered around the same three attributes: connecting, simplifying, and automating. Brand strategy and deep conceptual design thinking are what will make these brands stand out despite those inherent branding challenges.

They say, "Don't work harder, work smarter." Having a standard brand image will only make you work harder than those whose standout brands do some of the heavy lifting for them.

VISUAL CLARITY

If your brand has a strong logotype, refrain from using the same font as your main company font because it will only take away from the uniqueness and power of the logotype.

If you can't make a convincing business case for your rebranding, it is solely a waste of time and money.

VISUAL CLARITY

As a startup, you may feel like you don't have the time and money to care about branding. The truth is, you will be judged on your brand regardless of the effort you put in. So choose to make it as good as possible, just like everything else. It's what they expect and what you signed up for.

Consumers see user-generated content all day long. Don't be the brand that stands out as being too polished or too orchestrated. Professional, but 100% authentically you is the new human brand language.

VISUAL CLARITY

Creatives don't 'present work.' Instead, they recommend strategic solutions. As an industry, if we would change the lingo and subsequently live up to that promise, brands would not only be shaped faster but better.

Take note of new consumer brands you stumble upon during the week. Each Friday, allow yourself 30 minutes to dive into their sites and study the UX, brand voice, and design. Once Monday rolls around, you will realize how this simple exercise inspires your brand.

VISUAL CLARITY

Cultural and religious traditions often kill creativity in marketing and design. Don't let the step-and-repeat laziness within your country negatively affect your brand. Approach an old subject anew; surprise and delight, even on the same old occasion.

If brand cohesion is the desired outcome of a branding or rebranding project —which it always is—having a single person or team craft all designs simultaneously so one design can learn from or inform the other needs to be the desired process —which it rarely is.

VISUAL CLARITY

A logo needs to have legs; otherwise, you will carry the extra weight.

VISUAL CLARITY

Look and feel are much more than just that, and so are your brand's tone and voice. Both create brand clarity and are a part of what I like to call your brand atmosphere—that layer surrounding your offering that everyone needs to and, in the perfect case, wants to poke through to familiarize themselves with and hopefully end up buying into your offering and your brand as a whole.

VERBAL CLARITY

When providing feedback after creative design or copywriting presentations, do not say, "I like this" or "I don't like that." That's an opinion and is useless on its own. Instead, say, "I like this *because* it connects with [our strategy/audience/ brand direction] in X ways." Make your brand stronger and create better and faster results, all while making your creative team happy.

Imagination makes for good creative work. Editing transforms it into great work.

VERBAL CLARITY

Translate the essence of your social media strategy into content on your website. It will instantaneously portray your brand in an authentic way while being more engaging than your to-be-expected polished corporate site.

Want to test how well you know your customers? Off the top of your head, write down 10 frequently asked questions and correlating answers. They should be quirky, educational, delightful, and truly on brand. For great brands, this test should feel like telepathy—reading your customers' minds.

VERBAL CLARITY

Pick one:

I am you or we get you.

Then base your brand's copy and actions on those three words.

Would the brand name mmhmm make it through your naming focus group to be used for an app for professionals? How about Liquid Death for canned water from the Austrian Alps? These brands are killing it, and their standout names did their job. Mmhmm, lesson learned: death to naming focus groups!

VERBAL CLARITY

The purpose statement is the new manifesto.

Your brand name has every right to be lengthy, unusual, or flat-out weird as long as it fits your brand's personality and remains memorable.

VERBAL CLARITY

Having a descriptive brand name holding your company back is far worse than starting afresh with a creative name that will require initial marketing dollars and customer education.

*B2B brands ache to be more approachable, loveable, and human; in short, in tune with today's zeitgeist.
It's best to start that journey by disassociating your brand with terms that sound outdated, like webinar and e-book.*

VERBAL CLARITY

I am listening to Shopify and I use Spotify for eCommerce. Out the window goes the idea of only researching your direct competitors when naming your brand. Steer away from causing confusion, or simply frustration, if your proposed name is close to a well known brand with an overlap in audience.

Your sales team are brand marketers hidden in disguise. They have the ultimate knowledge of what your customers love about the company, enabling you to re-use your audience's words in order to get your brand in sync with how your customers actually see it.

VERBAL CLARITY

The best and cheapest way to stand out as a startup and turn into a brand? Have tons of attitude. It's what the bigger brands can't do but you can.

Be bold.
Be loud.
Be different.
Be radically transparent.
Be unapologetic.

It's free and it's yours if you have the guts to make it happen.

VERBAL CLARITY

RESOURCES

Scan for the latest brand insights and opportunities to learn from or engage with me.

Gain continuous branding insights and actionable advice: **FINIEN.COM/INSIGHTS**

Listen to conversations with founders about the intersection of brand clarity and startup success: **HITTINGTHEMARKPODCAST.COM**

Need swift, personalized brand advice? Schedule a brief call with me using Clarity. I would love to connect: **CLARITY.FM/FABIANGEYRHALTER**

Establish your brand platform through my online course: **ERESONAID.COM**

To work with me and/or my consultancy, FINIEN, on your brand strategy, name, or brand identity design or to book me for a workshop, panel, or speaking engagement, please email me directly at **FGEYRHALTER@FINIEN.COM**

FURTHER READING

OVERARCHING

THE BRAND THERAPY BOOK
by Fabian Geyrhalter

The first part of the book you just read.

HOW TO LAUNCH A BRAND
by Fabian Geyrhalter

Your step-by-step guide to crafting a brand:
from positioning to naming and brand identity.

BRAND STRATEGY

BIGGER THAN THIS
by Fabian Geyrhalter

A quick read about the deceptively difficult task
of turning your venture into an admired brand.

SCRAMBLE
by Marty Neumeier

The powerful tools at the center of this business thriller are the five Qs of strategy and the five Ps of design thinking.

VISUAL CLARITY

DESIGNING BRAND IDENTITY
by Alina Wheeler

Whether you're the project manager for your company's rebrand or you need to educate your staff or your students about brand fundamentals, *Designing Brand Identity* is the quintessential resource.

VERBAL CLARITY

ON PURPOSE
by Shaun Smith and Andy Milligan

Once you have defined your brand DNA, this book will assist you in defining and delivering your message of purpose to boost your customers' experiences with your brand and further instill it into your company's culture.

BRAND NAMING
by Rob Meyerson

The name is one of the first, longest-lasting, and most important decisions in defining the brand identity of a company, product, or service. If you are on a bootstrapped budget then Rob's book will be your guide to get you there successfully.

ABOUT THE AUTHOR

Fabian Geyrhalter, an acclaimed brand strategist and creative director, is the principal of Los Angeles–based brand consultancy FINIEN and a partner at Chameleon Collective, a business consultancy that in 2022 made the Inc. 5000 list of America's fastest-growing private companies for the second year in a row.

Fabian understands that any venture can turn into an admired brand if developed in an intrinsic, holistic, and methodological manner. He has deep expertise in guiding companies through their brand transformations and has been sought out by companies such as Marriott, Warner Bros., Match, Honeywell, Kaplan, and Randstad. His thoughts on branding have appeared in publications like Inc., Forbes, Entrepreneur, and The Washington Post, and his creative direction has won more than 50 international awards.

All three of his books became international Amazon Bestsellers and turned into go-to resources for entrepreneurs and marketers alike. From his Resonaid brand strategy workshops to the Hitting the Mark podcast where he talks to some of today's most prolific founders about brand strategy, Fabian is in a constant stimulation cycle, which is clearly visible when he advises clients or shares his insights with his followers or mentees. In 2022 he received the inaugural Global Startup Mentor Award for being the highest-rated mentor in the US by Founder Institute, the world's largest pre-seed accelerator.

Also in 2022, Fabian launched a product startup, Toneoptic, which brings innovation, coupled with his brand-thinking, to the vinyl record display space.